F. A. Sharhan is a young ambitious Emirati poet, writer, and multitalented artist. She holds a bachelor's degree in applied science (applied communication – applied media) from the Higher College of Technology in Ras Al-Khaimah. Since she was a little kid, Fatema enjoyed writing short-stories and poems in both Arabic and English languages.

Fatema is known for her strong personality; she is able to explain her thoughts to others and leave a mark on their minds. Fatema admires all forms of art and different cultures. She draws and paints sometimes, and she participated in two festivals in Ras Al-Khaimah with her artwork.

In memory of my late cousin

When we lost you,
we lost a huge part of ourselves,
a part that is difficult to replace.

***

To my parents

I am because of you
so, hold me tight always

***

To 'H'
My companion on the darkest journey

***

To my childhood friend 'A'

Because you believed in me,
this book started after that belief,
almost 20 years, and your friend is now here!

***

To my friend 'S'

My shining star
who always calls me 'Sea',
my deepest soul in your hands
so, thank you.

***

To the writer friend 'F'

Elegant in the form of words,
my all-time supporter.

***

To all my family, friends, and loved ones,
here's a piece from my heart,
here are the words,
running in my blood.

Love you all.

F. A. Sharhan

FIRE IN MY SOUL

AUSTIN MACAULEY PUBLISHERS™

LONDON • CAMBRIDGE • NEW YORK • SHARJAH

ISBN – 9789948794929 – (Paperback)
ISBN – 9789948794936 – (E-Book)

Application Number: MC-10-01-0438983
Age Classification: E

Printer Name: iPrint Global Ltd
Printer Address: Witchford, England

First Published 2023
AUSTIN MACAULEY PUBLISHERS FZE
Sharjah Publishing City
P.O Box [519201]
Sharjah, UAE
www.austinmacauley.ae
+971 655 95 202

This book holds the author's writings, emotions, and experiences from 2013 to 2021.

Table of Contents

Preface

Poems are the ego of a poet, a way to reveal emotions through them. The intention was to create a book that anyone can relate to because we all have different mindsets, personalities, and memories. In life, we have all been through many trials that only we know about. It's up to us to understand and unravel these words in a way that only we can relate to. We might have different perspectives and that's okay. Just imagine yourself in between every line, with every theme and poem.

Focus, Breathe, and Reflect

This book is meant to be understood by you as a reader. Encourage, define, and push you toward what's surrounding you. It's for you to make a connection within this inner circle. Far away from the outside world, and from what was originally intended.

If the writer's role is to capture life, then a reader's role is to search for meaning. And it's never a bad experience to search for that.

If it were that easy,
I would put my whole life,
into a book,
but it isn't,
more than two decades,
can't fit it, can't encase it,
I may also be scared,
to lose,
some of the great memories,
that I don't want to forget.

Blaze

How can life be regrouped,
and organized?
After it's been dispersed,
and gone to waste?
Those friendships and relationships,
what insanity struck them?
They became,
incomprehensible,
unstable,
and susceptible,
to possibilities,
unimaginable.

All the words you learn,
your entire life,
become worthless,
when you lose your friend,
leaving you with more pain,
for years,
endlessly.

Always acknowledge the senses,
contemplate them,
don't wait for permission,
feeling alone is enough,
resistance or stability?
Your heart hurts badly,
full of great things,
that are not surfacing.
Know what the truth is,
right! even if it's wrong,
defrauding itself,
convincing otherwise,
intuition does not disappoint,
sore, but not afraid.

You are forced to stay strong,

Whatever it takes,
to come along,
you are not even allowed,
to weaken or to hold back,
not to sing a song!
This is not a choice but a test.
You have difficulty unfeeling
what's happening,
an anxious silence,
prevails over you,
you sit quietly to rest,
on a bundle of your nerves,
waited all-day,
staring too long,
drowning.

Ironically, you are too persistent,

Trying to entrench yourself,
in the depths of your ground,
everyone thinks that nothing,
can fold, twist or break you,
while you are from the inside,
broken, folded and swung,
completely powerless!

I wished they could see,
I'm not made of steel,
broken inside,
and how much pain I feel,
while I'm overly persistent,
and feign strength,
continuing to live my life,
and yet, I feel lonely without them,
are my feelings even real?

Yesterday
I started singing,
even as,
I was whining,
I swear to God,
it's as if
the pains inside
are killing me
of oppression!

I'm going through this phase,
with no clue, with no chase,
being visible is tiring and fake,
invisibility is a power, like the air,
like perfumes, like the joy of love,
like the agony of grief!

Sorrows have varieties,
yet we may feel them at once.
At night they start hunting,
attacking people like me and you,
lurking around those who are in pain,
hearing the sorrow,
and you'll know,
some you could talk about,
as much as the sadness go,
and some you can't even explain!

As for the difference that cannot bear,
it's the sorrow of the loved ones,
yet hands are not enough to heal,
the friend's circle of grief widens,
furious and well aware,
of the meaning of pain,
that pushes a person to run away,
to sleep, or even waking up long,
such a bad condition,
how can words remain immortal,
in a sad chest, full of pains,
and overwhelmed,
with an endless number of words?
The stamina is coming to an end,
and the eyes sunk in the wrench,
still resilient and repressed,
been too discreet, distressed and exhausted,
does not know what choice to make,
couldn't stop arguing with life,
it makes no difference,
so read again
from the very first line!

To nobody,
I'm also nobody,
deviating despite my integrity,
smiling despite my melancholy,
heart filled with ache,
grief aching my ribs,
no lights, no tricks
standing in a dark place,
fearful,
hearing the echoes of my own disquietude,
and you never heard mine,

Dear nobody,
I have become very afraid,
standing amidst everything,
completely dazed,
by the accumulation of sorrows
thinking about the way it arose,
never fading away,
together they're saved,
there is no room for more,
neither a path to escape.

Sometimes we build,
a graveyard within our souls,
for all the things in life,
that die within us!

How long have I been,
waiting for you?
And now finally,
your nostalgia,
has brought you!
Where have those feelings been?
Where were you?
Autumn leaves fallen,
for you,
for a laugh from your lips,
my poem was a sight,
but the reality is blind!
Don't wave at me,
like someone leaving,
I'm possibly angry
of being quite guilty
but the presence of your absence,
erased all the consequences from
whatever fate has woven for me.

Give me a moment,
I want to have,
anything from our old times,
I swear I want,
to fill that spot,
left empty inside!
Okay, hello?
I want to,
console my ears,
neither can I express in words,
nor understand my crime!
I know to you
I am unimportant,
nor a lover!
But could I ever recover?
And be happy with another?

Was born in a storm,
lightning in the soul,
thunder in the heart,
and chaos in the bones.
Half of what people say
was meaningless,
you just want to stay away,
from all of this,
but where is the deliverance?
Keep thinking,
how can a person be,
so sane and yet
scattered inside?

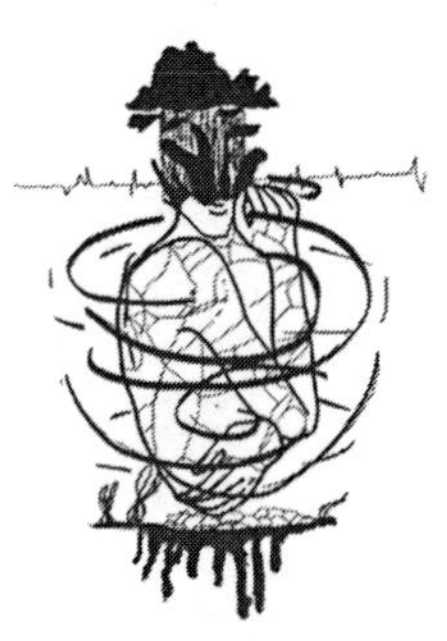

I might be complicated,
I admit that,
like waves of blue ocean,
recumbent on a rocky shore.
I learned some lessons,
with many distractions,
I know the difference,
and the smell of deceit,
what's an illusion?
And what is life about?
What are dreams and how to
walk towards them?
A piece of advice
I may give you at last,
never live a life in the past!

29

You reach a stage in life,
unable to participate,
even with a word,
convinced that it's the best, to,
become a spectator,
without igniting.
Because you don't disclose,
they think you don't care,
It's just a play of roles,
of powers,
over your own,
devastation!

We had a fight,
on Friday night,
I waited four months,
but it's been years already,
and Saturday morning
never comes.
It's been years
how many
nights and days
how many
moons and suns
already!

Spends a lot before sleeping,

Sparkly thoughts,
attached by dreams,
the truth it seems,
not how it feels,
the way is long,
impossible to flee,
my pillow is filled with perplexity,
the throat of mine crowded with words,
been underestimated in this world,
owe nothing to anyone,

Like the sea,

A diver in it does not see,
how deep it can be!

I believe in what I saw
when I dreamed of you
enough of this agony
of waiting for you,
I became unaware of you
after I was fully aware.
If I close my eyes,
how much nearer you can be
yet how far away,
in my dream, I became
a king above his throne,
I blink, and I'm afraid
to lose you in that,
I fear that if I open my eyes
I will never meet you again.

Oh postman,

I have a letter
I wish it could reach its destination,
I wish you could deliver,
but I do not have
their new address,
and I haven't heard
any good tidings from them.

Oh postman,

Help me figure this out,
can you take my words,
with my whispers?

Arrived somewhere in life,
telling yourself that
it smashed you endlessly
you have seen many,
lived sadness and frailty,
it's never too late to get back up,
walk towards a destiny,
while others may reach it without any,
you were the hero, your dream knight,
and that awaited savior,
you fought for every right
with a privilege in your life,
you fought to find a chance,
to be a cinematic hero in every scene,
you have long dreamed about.
You took care of yourself,
while half of these here,
didn't dare to care.
No shoulder to rest on,
trying to tear you apart
as if the road was erased
that from which I came,
turned but couldn't stop,
tired to walk, with no guide,
nevertheless, found
a hidden pleasure
and something that mattered
after all that has passed,
why were you in a scene,
if no one had even noticed?

Who turned you off?
Brought back into the dark,
and tore you apart!

Who will apologize
about the scars,
life has seared,
onto our souls!
About the fires,
that are lit inside,
our minds,
by the fools!
Everyone knows,
it's hard,
isn't worth
the apologies!

The fragrance of some memories,
makes me nauseous and dizzy.
It hurts, and
cuts my breath short,
bound by the guilt with chains.

The night just fell,
I heard a whisper,
my coffee machine,
and the beans,
both calling me,
"Darling, come take a sip,"
coffee beans are my heart,
crushed by you my friend
when I held the cup near,
a question was in the air:
"If I pour coffee for you,
what will you pour for life?"
Leaving me with my thoughts
hard pressed,
drinking coffee endlessly,
and a mind tied up in knots.

Life keeps opening old wounds
I'm not pouring it anything.

Have you ever felt that feeling? When you feel like you have forgotten something somewhere, but you don't know what it is, perhaps because you forgot yourself. A while ago I felt that, and I think I have forgotten myself in a place. I don't know where to find it.

The danger is you,
and the words are
fraught with you,
or perhaps,
you are the abyss,
and I am on your edge,
with all the other things
within my existence!

There was neither,
a stab, nor a scab,
there were no coincidences,
that embraces our meetings.

Trust me when I say,
nobody properly cared,
if you left,
carrying their shortcomings,
painfully in the heart,
ignoring all the things
can't find any apologies.
walking on roads of sarcasm,
and inside the head,
a mockery of logic,
no one can keep up with.

Inferno

A friend of mine once told me that people's attributes, morals, and behaviors are gray. Our behaviors aren't just white or black… sometimes our white qualities overwhelm the black, and sometimes our black qualities overwhelm the white.

The curtains lift
the stage is set,
people are killed,
others are crying,
the crowd applauds,
dramatic scenes play along.

The doors are slammed shut!

It would be so scary,
to be fully deactivated,
as if you're a kind of machine,
while you're very angry,
hiding that ugly voice,
inside the mind of yours,
to stray,
then where will you be found?

There are people in life with whom our relationship isn't important or of interest, but there was a sincere love from the heart that we recognize when we miss them, even when we barely knew them.

It was so tempting,
to do everything with you,
like the redemption of a soul,
splitting into two,
I still feel that elation,
weal, woe, or sorrow,
shared all expressions,
light or shadow,
as if our union,
was a map towards home,
with a thousand roads,
that lead to Rome.

God decreed,
that we be friends,
we have been thrown,
onto the same road,
perhaps for a certain purpose that,
we may not grasp.
I will always grab your hand,
if you ever fell and,
when you suffer,
I will never gloat.
I'm sorry if I've ever been,
too weak to lean on,
too miserable to support,
when you needed me the most,
the only fear is that,
we don't know when,
one of us will die,
nor how the other will,
move on without the other.
I'm sorry again,
knowing you very well,
and the troubles there,
that you don't share,
you really have tried,
not to show it,
but I have seen.

Stare into the abyss,
seeing your specter,
appearing just like this,
how much more horrifying
can it get?
You don't even exist,
this is a crime,
and you are the punishment,
the friend that I miss and so,
may you rest,
forever in bliss.

My old sad words,
have no longer hurt me,
what's hurt the most,
is the escaping idea,
from the bitter reality of the world,
it became painful for me,
and I never found the way
to the end,
or salvation.

You'll never know,

How sorrow feels,
till you lose,
your closest one,
the deepest soul,
the dearest friend,
your very own,
the only one,
in this world.

Like rain was his voice,
watering my heart after long grief,
like a roof over life,
steady on the wound,
imagine the waste,
of my empty days,
can't stand this crushing grief,
on my own, in the gloom,
life dead inside my eyes,
and the soreness is great,
greater than the capacity,
of my endurance!

You look so sad

Your expressions
deathly
a nostalgia
what remains
of the those who
pass us by
you're searching
for a face
just like your own
very sad.

Yes, I am sad,

Searching around
into the souls
for a person like me
exactly the same
I need a lot more
than a face
I need to become myself,
and have my greatest feelings of joy
surrounding me
but I'm now
lost in sorrow.

How can you,

Fall asleep,
after you were blamed!
I hadn't given you,
except some of what I have,
how could you starve me?
Leaving my chest full of words.
Such an unjust person,
it was so unfair to me,
I have stolen for you,
a thing from everything,
if you had just asked,
I could've brought you,
the heads of clouds!
If only you wanted to,
I was going to be to you,
a ray of sunlight!

Oh, my dear darling!

I do not even greet,
all those after you,
what is this thirst that I have reached?
After your separation,
the whole universe is looking,
I cannot find words,
telling you that I was,
so broken after you!

Feeling heavy,
on this sleepy heart,
a bit unsteady
overlooking those wounds,
healing already,
an unbalanced heartbeat,
carried by sadness,
and an absence,
in the middle of the road,
I became a person,
I don't know anymore,
with an iron heart,
patient but always alone.

Grief is a gust,
that refuses to leave us,
and makes it hard to forget,
people you shared with,
many memories and laughs.

Knocking on their doors,
knowing perfectly, they've left,
that sick soul knows it as well,
wishing that they had fallen,
before those tears ever fell,
the tears are great,
and the feelings hidden
behind them,
are greater!

Looking up at the night,
with bloodied sleepless eyes,
and weighted eyelids,
feel suspicious of what
will follow,
the heart starts moaning
from wounds and delusions,
everyone left and repelled it
needs to rest,
needs inspiration, goals, and dreams
once it believes in itself
it can take spontaneous risks,
the past is a page,
and we all reach to it!
The word is a weapon,
and they all betrayed with it!
No one ever lasted,
neither a single dearest,
nor who has an interest,
says they've been bartered,
well, now they forced him,
to take cruel paths
after all those times!
They're just betraying!

a big guardian among them,
whose presence is honored,
no doubt is admissible,
by all these who tried,
to lead him to the execution!

Dying is so majestic,
to sense what death means,
the death of places, the death of things,
or even how life dies,
while you are still alive,
everyone thinks,
you have overcome the feelings,
of losing someone close,
but you are pulled back,
with every new loss,
to that day and to that exact time,
hearing the clock,
tick-tock.

Shivering, thinking about,
how do I tell you about life,
after you left?
Or even about,
the days, good and bad,
passing with no rays of sunlight,
and what those years have been like
and the people who have passed?
Or that house,
that is no longer as delightful as
how it's been,
and how it became after you?
Or that hurting heart,
didn't cry a thing
like your grief,
losing you was sadness,
with many tears.

My trees are lonesome,

Wanting to lead birds,
throw branches apart,
to bend over your fields,

In vain,

I guided them,

In vain…

Trying to sing your name!

Some paths I took
I walked…
with nobody alongside me,
I drowned…
I groaned…
and it consumed me,
too much to care about,
too much to step aside from,
everyone wanted your light,
but no one can handle your ashes!

Among us,
there are killers,
who've never made a mess,
or ever shed blood!
They're hustlers,
all they do,
is hold your
hurting limbs,
they never dare
to get close,
to your dead borders!

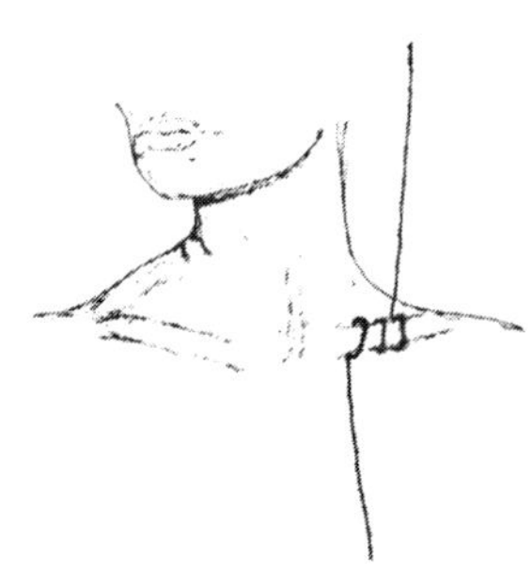

There is a word,
buried in the center of my chest,
if I said it, it would show,
how broken I am!
And if I keep it hidden,
it will hurt!
Oh, killer,
I wish you were here,
and you could feel this treachery!

Lived life with
disappointments,
in a disgusting way!
Cannot forgive nor
forget easily,
with a lot of
convictions,
and philosophies,
cannot find anyone
who understands,
other than itself,
cannot interact nor
make a pact,
with the world!

Have been marred by the days,
in a distant past,
my life passes,
the yearning increases,
I'm forced by time,
I wish it would change!

So alone and terrified,
for years,
bowed that head,
the flower cried,
I saw its tears!
Without lights
to guide,
or fears,
whispering in their ears,
not your turn to decide,
the spirit passed
from inside
feeling pride!

A beautiful night,
but the moon is sad,
I can feel it here,
through its reflection,
watching it,
without approaching,
it is confused
lonely,
staring at earth.
How sad is that,
to see the moon,
so alone!

The morning was drawing for me
spectra and dreams,
and now it's no longer,
working for me.

It's died

That feeling
that I wanted to share,
years ago!
They've died

The roses,
I've been holding,
for so long,

So strong!

Will time ever pass?
I'll remember that night forever,
fearing the feeling, upsetting
and have emotions filling,
the truth is bitter and I'm afraid,
to face it alone with my tears
will it ever be answered?
No, not in a hundred years!
Bring the words and speak openly,
because I'm thinking in hyperbole,
I frankly don't have time.
Without verses, there'll not be poems,
the fracture within, must not be shown,
the poet should balance it all!
Look at the point of this role,
along with peace of soul,
the greed falls on its owner,
will time ever pass or never?
I am the one who sits and waits,
to bid farewell forever.

It is only once,
seeing the world,
riding your thoughts,
fading away,
falls within you what used to be great,
everything else falls from your eyes
just as autumn leaves fell,
contradicting your feelings
causes a lot of pain and suffering.
Feel the urge to consume dullness,
with a cold cup of indifference,
the world is bad, not realizing the size
of your own expectations,
does not pay it any attention,
cause as the actor plays
a romantic play,
the world wants him
to represent it every day.

Feelings suddenly flowing,
facts penetrate with infinite meanings,
thoughts awaken, questions crowded
and answers get scattered,
running in fear, and then crying about this road,
panting, not able to continue walking,
the sky is far, a frightening noise, and fierce pain,
an incoming hurricane,
erupting volcanoes, collapsing towers,
floods of seas and rivers.
A majestic crowd,
screaming, clamoring,
the city never shut out,
things in life are fatal,
body static, features calm,
nothing was connected anyway,
it was not how it was meant to be,
trying to slow the feelings from flowing,
finding them leaking…and drowning!

Believing can't convince fate
feeling sorrow,
thinking of tomorrow,
surrounded by fools,
and implicated,
no longer wanting more relationships,
increasing those,
means more disappointments and losses.
No longer strong enough to confront,
even those who are gone forever,
could not say farewell,
hoping for their return,
and waiting,
they are not coming back
leaving you confused, wondering,
do I keep an infected arm?
Or do I amputate it?

People are different,
their different personalities,
how hard it is to break their habits!
And all the ways they express things,
all so diverse,
the only un-different thing is,
People are all alike,
in death.

Shivering, while the long road folds,
in the heart,
takes it back to the past,
to that song,
to the first time we heard it
me and you
to when I'm watching a movie,
that I had seen for the first time
with you
or to be sitting somewhere,
where we came before!
They're gone,
all these sweet moments
with you,
they're gone,
regrettably,
with you,
without a farewell, or a word.
They're gone,
with you, becoming a memory.

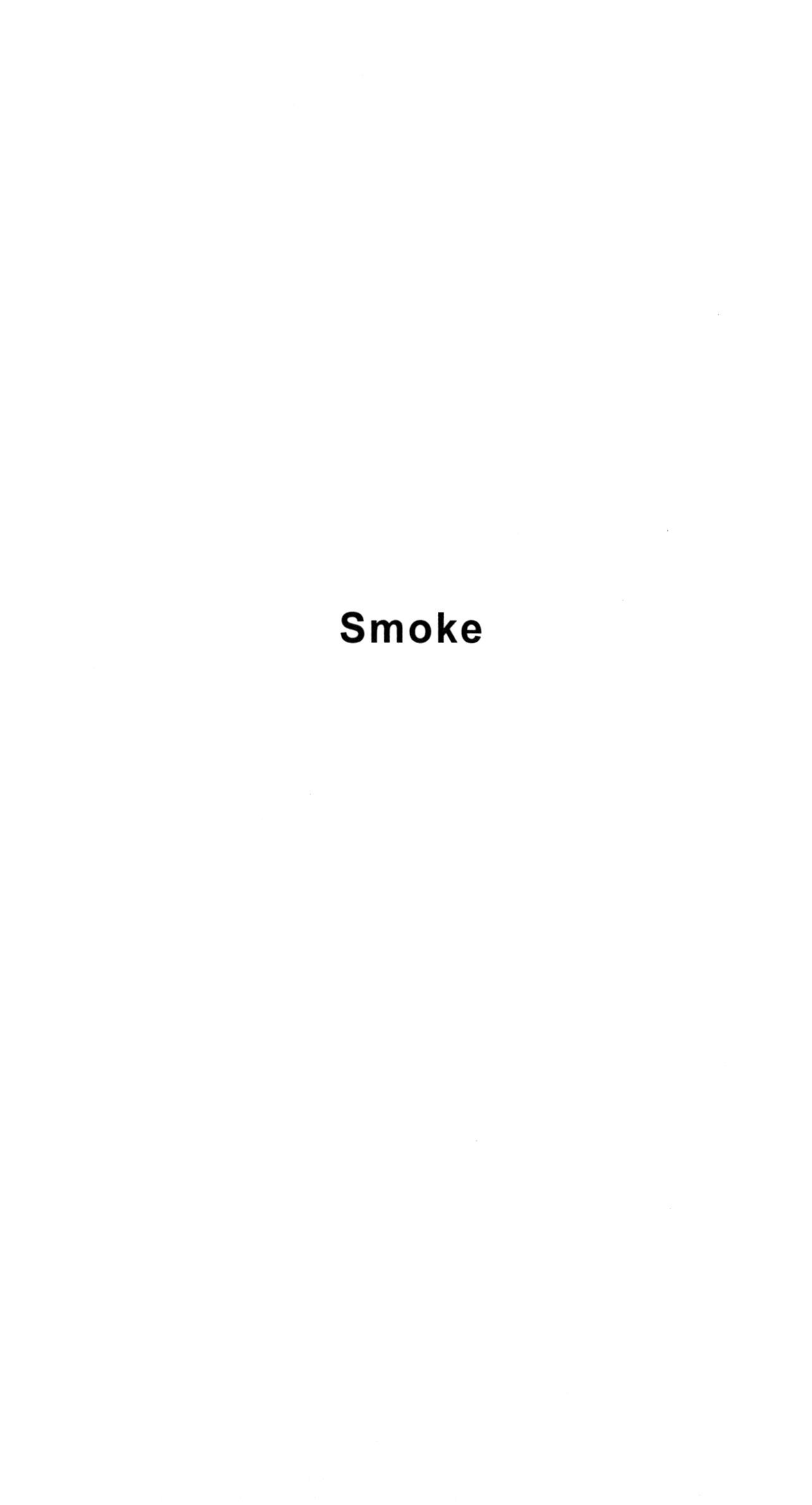

Smoke

The rays of the morning sun smile at him, he puts on a face unlike his own. The look of the new day wakes him, he hides the past under his pillow, stuffing as much as possible of his feelings, into his pockets, ensures the integrity of his thoughts, leaning on the crutches of his crumbling dreams, coming out, to fight the battle, at the center of life's juncture. His slender bones are shattered, the sounds run over him, yet he's still holding up. Hopes that life will be as they told him, find it completely different, not what's been expected. This happens every day. But he's still resilient. It's ironic of fate that everything you make is pointless and useless. Solutions move away, tears fall, thoughts sneak into the darkness to disappear, problems haunt him, and death is destined. He has no power to fall, so he continues to walk in. "Run-away!" Run like runners, life will not fall with you, and the world will not be destroyed if you ever stopped.

Tall and high, towards the sky,
like the trees standing by,
cruel and hard like the stones,
like the mountain, fixed pillars,
and like the winds that carry,
both my aromas and my breaths.

Around us,
Different eyes,
Different people,
Different stories.

We shared a name,
we shared a town,
you were always there,
inspiring me to change,
I can see now,
above the clouds,
you let my wings grow,
so I could fly and,
together we became like,
an extraordinary lightning bolt.

You are to me,
not just a friend,
you are different,
like ribs that protect my heart,
a shield surrounding it.
a land to call home.
And you are to me,
not just a friend,
you are my soul,
to which I run,
from the world,
and myself!

You were the one who found me,
when life set out to defeat me,
venturing, to hear my voice,
and see me laugh,
emanating from me,
forgiving my mistakes,
never blaming my mood swings,
quelling my sorrows,
when I don't even know,
we conquered life together,
years back,
when you existed!

I wanted to,
but I couldn't
then separation
became
optional
we didn't get along,
but it's okay…
God will bless fate,
and God will make it be.

You're a stranger to me,

As I am to you,
let me understand
and you may try it too,
be close to my heart,
and slowly touch my soul.

What are you looking for?

And what am I?
Bridge this together,
at any cost,
so simultaneously
we could be.

A friend of mine just told me that,
she's been delightful she's been on track,
once upon a time she fell in love,
everything just went, so wrong,
a question was looming in the sky,
am I the sinner? Am I the lover?
Who am I?

I see you stalking me,
I stalked you too!
I went there first,
I picked you alone,
to me, you shall come,
and I should for you!
As far as it begins,
we must be one soul.

Walking between the hands of life,
balancing its scale,
but it makes us hesitant,
and we still try to overcome,
rebelling in critical moments,
as if there is nothing,
between us and her,
recklessly…
If we fell,
or our dreams were shattered!
Farewell,
getting lost within the wheels of life,
never finding our stations!
Full of hope,
we wish we were birds,
so we could spread our wings,
flying freely,
but we can't,
we can only breathe out,
to fly these beautiful thoughts.

Who said love comes after enmity?
If it was, it'll not be affected,
with reflecting that feeling,
or that should be alerted,
I mean, like what's been said,
hate may come after loving!

Sometimes,
I like to be alone,
thinking to the bone,
I see a different world,
with a sweet melodious tone,
through eyes and ears,
and no worries or fears.

I always stayed,
at the end of it all,
whether those endings are,
happy or sour.
I'm not the one to initiate
ending relationships
in my life,
the characters bow,
and the masks are taken off,
just like that,
for no real reason,
with no justifications,
yet I am,
always there,
since the beginning,
to the ending,
you will find me saying goodbye
with a smile or a laugh,
you have to choose the end,
it's in your hand.

We all got punished,
and beaten by life,
that's why
we understand
each other
so well.

If you regret this silence,
I regret it too!
Come back and we'll
fix everything
together!

You're in me,
in the deepest part of me,
deeper than my memories,
and my thoughts.
Yet you didn't see.

You chose to cross,
the sea of life,
without hesitation,
without foreseeing,
the dangers to come your way.

I'm broken, losing my way,
if my fate is not by my side,
I no longer know how to stay,
to be good and kind,
watchful or advanced,
I know that I have been
cold as the clay,
not shining every day.

Oh, rare precious gem,
believe me when I say,
you're always on my mind,
don't lead me astray.

Be busy,
till you don't have any
time left, to look back,
at your past,
take your heart,
and every inch of you,
with all your feelings, and pains,
turn it into a story, into art,
into something that's worth it,
to fight, your days' wars
something you are
proud to look at,
for this,
don't you ever,
never, ever
give up,
battle,
with all your strength,
you deserve that!

Do whatever you thought impossible,
walking like a stranger,
among old friends,
don't care if nobody stops to greet,
despite all the situations,
or how you've been treated,
you have ever been through,
your feelings are instilled,
then taken away immediately,
your soil is patient,
no longer fertile,
for the complex roots you have,
making you contradictory,
despite your strength,
a word can make you sad,
another can please you for long.

Don't owe a thing in life,

Silence is an objection.
Sadness seeps from your heart,
making some connection,
to voice and facial features!
Lying no longer works,
that you are just fine,
solely through affection,
the greatest you would be.
O tilted branch, always

Grow but never,
leave your tree.

I don't know my value
in your heart,
I want to ask,
but I am afraid,
I'm like the dream to you,
and dreams are magical!
If you admire it,
answer and exchange letters!
Is it so ridiculous?
Or is it in your heart,
with no alternatives?

In life, we meet a lot of people
some that we never forget about,
they are never really ours,
but they show us the stars,
and what living feels like,
some things we thought of,
some we never think about!
How can things be shining,
but not with us
they shift their decreed desires,
showing us a flowered path,
in another way of fate,
they feel like soulmates!
Living a different life within,
never close or far,
not fair enough even to us,
to keep them in mind,
never knowing for real,
where they really are?

A conversation going,
you've been told,
hear your inner voice,
no excitement, no encouragement,
deep thoughts tire the one,
but they can't understand it,
their thinking is superficial,
never walk with the flock,
be aware you're different,
and you'll be criticized,
especially when you reach high peaks,
like when action rises at the climax then falls,
they might think a person can't fly,
or they may think you should stay aside,
watching them fly away, they fear that
if you come, you'll fly high,
it's better for them if you're,
a broken-winged bird, blown through the wind
silence is a cure sometimes.
Fall once, twice, and a hundred times
be sad and cry by yourself,
when you are successful,
no one will be able to affect you.

To save myself,
I had to wreak havoc,
but I'm not ready for another battle,
to bring back what once existed,
but I'll never be a loser,
never show my abuser,
that I no longer
have any space,
to be decisive,
I just really don't care,
All my feelings were taken
by disappointment,
restoring stability
these are the rules of life.
And if you want something
emotionally, first
your pride must be put to death.

She might seem off but she's an art,
can leave you standing facing the wall!
Without you, she falls apart,
without her, you're nothing at all!
Does that change anything at heart?
Or does it mean the sky would fall?

Afraid to talk,
because talking can destroy things,
talking causes misfortunes,
it is half lost, and half fog,
the fog, when it rises, causes a crisis.
Doesn't leave a conscious mind,
talking can cause disasters,
demolish and trigger predicaments,
talking can cause separations,
estrangement among friends,
doesn't leave ill-will out of hearts,
and the heart becomes so weak,
waiting for something to seek,
softly, so calm and meek
the heart doesn't think of love,
neither thinks about speech,
the heart only wants life,
to walk the way, it wants to live.

Why should I be afraid?
there is nothing left to fear,
without avail,
I was afraid,
to stay away,
distanced,
from the world…
It was my only fear!
And I got it…
I am far away!
There's no need,
to be afraid,
not anymore,
I am away, far away!

Nobody knows,
about your little fights,
how sleep was
forced on you,
nor how you
convince yourself,
by drawing all these
blameless expressions
on your face,
your little fights are organized,
your victories are very private,
perhaps trivial,
but it is a perfect way,
to keep fighting,
through life,
every day.

I said that I will come back
rehearsing words days before,
years of remorse after suffering,
as I grew much rougher,
wishing that we were together
can you even come back to us?
Catch those arranged words,
days passed by,
the heart contains them
in the gloom,
as the years go on and on,
as if it was tortured,
nobody asks how it is,
nobody will feel its sorrow.
It may not have loved you first,
but it'll always love you the most!

Lucky you, if you have ever,
been loved by an artist or a writer,
imagine these two combined,
in one person that becomes your lover,
lucky you!

Might my name be defeated,

Or defeat took its name from me,
but I always survive,
whatever the scale
of the pain formed
within my heart
blown in the form of a sigh,

I survive!

Whatever the volume of speech
lingering at the edge of my throat
refusing to leave,

I survive!

Even if I do not understand
the scale of the tragedy
that befell with all its weight
on my shoulders

I survive!

We race against the weather
and we race with the clouds
the sun is shining brighter
while it races and passes by
our thoughts become lighter
going through some struggle
and surviving with no trouble
to learn that
even if we could too
race against the wind
we will never give in
staying as a fighter,
till we win.

As the sun kisses the face,
kisses the window,
and on the floor made a trace,
it loved you much,
it adores you more,
knowing that it would fail!
But it shall be taken to you
to meet in a hallowed place,
what a wonderful terminus
to bowing in the knees
full of happiness!

In this house and that,
even grandma's house,
I find places accommodating a lot,
of your gaze, your absent gait,
your laugh, your conversations, and jokes,
all of them will always remain,
can be seen, can be felt close,
this is a consolation,
your way isn't
and will never be erased.

Ashes

You were my entire audience

That never got bored
of sitting around,
through the theater of life
applauding me warmly
even when I was wrong.

You were my world

Who I always thought,
I would never move on from,
that I would ever say goodbye to,
as if you never were.

I know that "contentment is a treasure," but I don't have it. Everyone I've ever known pulled their hands away from mine. Friends became older, memories got colder, and every moment just passed along. I wasn't a barrier, but they turned me into a high dam. I left quietly, convinced. I don't care who followed, nor who would perish. Except for that companion, with whom I shared weal and woe. That one didn't betray our days, our memories, my tears. Always by my side and never against, whenever life pulled us apart, came back to hold my hand. All talk is temporary, even if it lasts, and all responses are lacking, compared to what I have. I've gathered all my feelings, to be given to my companion. Hopefully, we meet again. Hopefully.

Oh, my sleepy heart,

Who falls asleep on its wounds,
who does not want to wake up,
on a medicine that is not his!

Oh, my sleepy heart,

Who's afraid to suffer,
from a separation,
or to even live in,
the memory of the dead!

She was sad,
in her deepest thoughts,
but this kind of sadness,
gives hopes,
this kind,
that takes time!

You were her other soul,
and now you've left!
She can't find,
peace in her mind,
She might run away,
but there's no place to find!
And nowhere to go,
and nowhere to hide.
The memories begin to flow.
now she's looking for a place,
to restart through,
by finding her peace.

Do not be surprised,
by the smile or frown,
nor by the thoughts,
nor by the words,
sometimes it feels like,
you're tough on yourself
a heavy character,
that's hard to shake,
does not share feelings,
saying that the fatigue inside,
turned the scales,
but knowing very well,
how can a person,
heal by himself!

The distance tears me apart,
between our homes,
the longer it grew, I cried!
Our wishes and aspirations,
the consolation that we might die,
from longing,
will the distance even try,
to bring us together?

Ironically, we could fight for something.
Landing on other shores,
to lose everything else we had,
reaching fragile states,
that are nothing like us,
never are we the same again,
life steals many parts from us,
one to be found here, another there,
leaving parts of us everywhere,
you remain accepting of the person you are,
for as long as you'll be alive,
then at some point, you are
defeated by that very familiar voice
to your ears,
the tone beats you,
reluctantly turned,
despite the apparent
confusion in your eyes,
silence resolved, it wasn't him,
it sounds like his voice, but isn't
how can a voice bring you back to zero?
How can the years make a difference?
How can that very familiar voice,
bring you out of your exile?

Like a stranger you are,
coming to settle
and that sound is your ticket,
even together, they couldn't
for a few minutes, leave you alone,
in that cemetery in front of his gravestone,
the memories invaded and cursed you to the bone.
The city is without lights,
Its sky is pale,
an old house was left in my heart,
without a key,
good and bad news,
no one here to share it with,
no one to tease.
Years passed,
how fast!
Questions ate all of that
everything, small or vast
minds and hearts,
bones and even days.

Sometimes I feel,
I want to nap,
to forget
no pain, no hidden soreness,
sometimes I feel,
I want to wake
mistaken,
loving things,
even if they don't,
love me back.
Suffocating,
as if the whole world is,
asleep on my chest!
I had a memory pass by,
destroyed everything inside me,
and I was about to cry,
I had forgotten!
My dreams were my world,
until reality passed by,
and demolished them,
if you ever have the way,
never be the dependent, always the provider,
whoever collects memories, will live like me!

Wondering and amazed
what's it like to be told,
"you look a bit afraid"
like the golden hour,
of the afternoon,
a star when it gleams,
overcoming darkness,
sinking into grief,
whispering their names,
with a hope to liberated,
born into emptiness,
learning to be seen!

Hiding the end in my pocket,
and under my pillow,
since the beginning,
lacking the desire to continue living,
a passion inside,
didn't come alive,
far away. Can't reach it.

A volcano erupted in the chest,
neither water
nor patience, nor friends, could help
walking to my funeral
every day, empty.

Life passes on,
and doesn't pass,
it is complete,
but incomplete!
Many fires on my chest,
that the world can't accept.

I've never wanted to be,
a plan B
the alternative or the backing track,
but I've always felt,
like that unwanted weight,
the meal with no flavor,
the time that goes to waste,
the surplus of things along.
I mimic the world that I am,
steadfast but I'm destroyed,
can you build a broken wing?
How do you heal a single wound?
Have you had an actual friend?
Or have they been deceitful?
Is hell that soft to them?
Are they even afraid of the end?

In the sea of life,
you should try,
to swim or dive,
if you don't even know,
either of these two,
then you're responsible,
for your own drowning,
life will not go on,
teaching you the same lesson,
you must've learned to swim,
without drowning.

Eventually, they will know who I was
that's clear enough; although
eventually,
every one of them will know,
I am the best, and this is not because,
some idiot made the laws.

I'm a tropical storm in a row,
whose rings its claws,
seeking the glory and the glow,
not knowing when to pause.

Oh my dear,
not all the faces
deserve love,
some are dark places,
no matter what the case,
or what they are above,
the expression of grimaces,
you'll just not be able,
to feel it by any graces.

Life does not give lessons
free of charge,
never!
It may take
a lot of things
away from you,
to just teach you
one lesson.

Obey and be dutiful,
life is beautiful,
just be careful,
where to look,
because it's not
written in a book!
and which way
you may take,
trying to stay alive.

How are you so calm?
Tell me how the universe,
exists out of nowhere?
And tell me why do worms,
dig into graves?
What does the universe even mean?
How is it still unchanged?
While we changed!

And why do we end up,
without any memories?

I am searching,

For what is left for me,
of feelings!

I am searching,

As if it was lost
in a fire,
I don't know until when,
I'll almost be a half poet,
representing his glory,
in my poems!

All that is inside my mind, but I don't say, teach me that:
Neither people's words are silver, nor is my silence gold.

And God willing,
to divert the direction and flow
of this heart, from you,
to hate you in a deep way,
it does not belong to anyone,
single and alone!

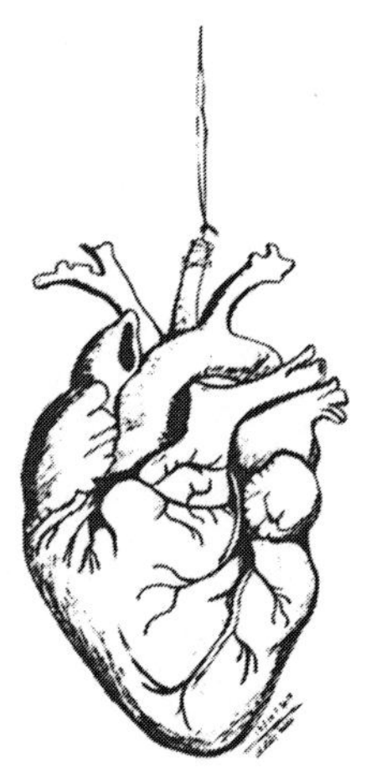

Like tree leaves, I fall,
knowing my time of sadness,
realizing that my destiny,
wilts in silence,
with a great pallor,
letting my poems slowly,
make the decisions for me,
forgiving the companions,
for what it was,
and what it is!
I'm about to be,
a portrait, and a name,
without features!
A song without
any feelings or wings!

Sometimes I stay up
thinking of
all the places
that reminds me
of all the people
that are gone.

Nobody knows you personally better than you do. Don't take things too seriously. And don't feel exposed, or pretend to be a mystery, treat everyone one way, nobody knows you as you really are. Feel the imperfections, everyone around you is imperfect too, stick to contentment, nobody ever looks the same anyway, don't think too much, and leave parts of you in everything you do. It seems like there are no parts of you left, but these are what represent you if combined, the world has never failed anyone, we are the ones who let the world down every time we give up our visions. Do not expect anything, amaze yourself by yourself, with what you can do, and do what you cannot, the attempt is a guide to success, you will seek salvation from the world, and it will not save you. When you enjoy it, it will bid you farewell, sometimes you will feel chained up, but the key is not with anyone but you, you are strong, full of words and emotions overflowing, paying attention to the smallest details and but no creases on your forehead, your pain is only yours, and your crying is not a sign of weakness, you're a contradiction between you and yourself.

Tik, tok
that's my clock
been at it looking
all day
before knocking
knock…knock
come let's talk
or if you prefer
to have a walk
around the block
what to even talk about
I had no words to say
mind a million miles away
rusty thoughts that need to be locked,
sometimes memories
brought me back
dressed in black
harder and tougher
than a rock
the louder they knock
the harder they crack
and I seem like a fool
now what will get me back
on the right track?

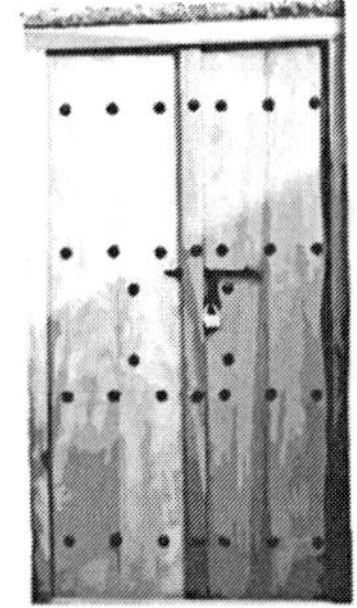

I sat within the darkness,
of my thoughts
the sound is loud,
usually, I sit quietly,
noticing the crowd's lips,
barely seeming natural,
beyond the cloud's mist,
something is missing,
become aloof as ever,
seeing life spinning infinitely.
I committed a lot of mistakes,
what happened? How was the battle?
The loss and struggle?
No one knew about it,
a sharp look, controversial,
invoked fear, hidden within,
what defeats the toughness,
not too forgetful, but so good at faking it.
Memories flow from every way,
tired of trying the whole day
arranging chaos, cleaning up intentions
between the mind and heart settling disputes,
extinguished eyes, inflamed soul,

seeking to survive,
even without control.

The day I begin to run,
I will leave everyone behind.
No more to be done,
nothing more in my mind,
it'll all be as past gone,
like a feather in the wind.

Survivor,
all the aches,
and memories,
pass through the lungs,
panting,
keep holding it,
half beautiful,
half sting.
Remaining dear,
to ourselves…
Even if it's wrong.

All my life I've wondered,
why say good-bye?
Like a suspended hour,
waiting without asking why,
moments never go under,
moments never fly.
Your blood is fire, I've been told,
flame or desire, I should hold
the wounds of life, are too old,
through a future, bright as gold.
In the end,
when the tired will mend,
and we finally see,
that we don't need to pretend,
I want just one thing,
to be satisfied
and have nothing to hide.